The Kid's Guide to

MAX
The Golden Retriever

Written by A.J. Richards   **Illustrated by Rayah Jaymes**

The Kid's Guide to Max the Golden Retriever

ISBN-13 : 978-1508840756
ISBN-10: 150884075X

Disclaimer: The information in this book does not replace a consultation with a veterinarian and/or a behavior consultant and may not be used to diagnose or treat any of your dog's conditions. Dog training is not without risks. When in doubt, consult a professional dog trainer or canine behaviorist. A.J. Richards cannot guarantee that your dog will instantly start to behave. Like anything in life, dog training requires work. Issues that arise could depend on many factors beyond our control, such as, the amount of time you are willing to invest in training your dog, your ability to apply what you have learned, and the possibility that your dog may have a rare genetic or health condition affecting his or her behavior. A.J. Richards cannot guarantee any method and is not liable in any case of sickness, injury, or death.

Book Cover and Design by Vermilion Chameleon Illustration and Design
www.vcartist.com

Printed in the U.S.A

"The price of greatness is responsibility."
– Winston Churchill

"Live life like a puppy, treat every day like an adventure!"
-Kid's Best Friend

This Book Belongs To:

_____

Your Name

_____

Your Dog's Name

Hello! My name is Maxwell, but my friends call me Max.
I am a **Golden Retriever**. Would you like to hear my story?

I was born in Scotland.

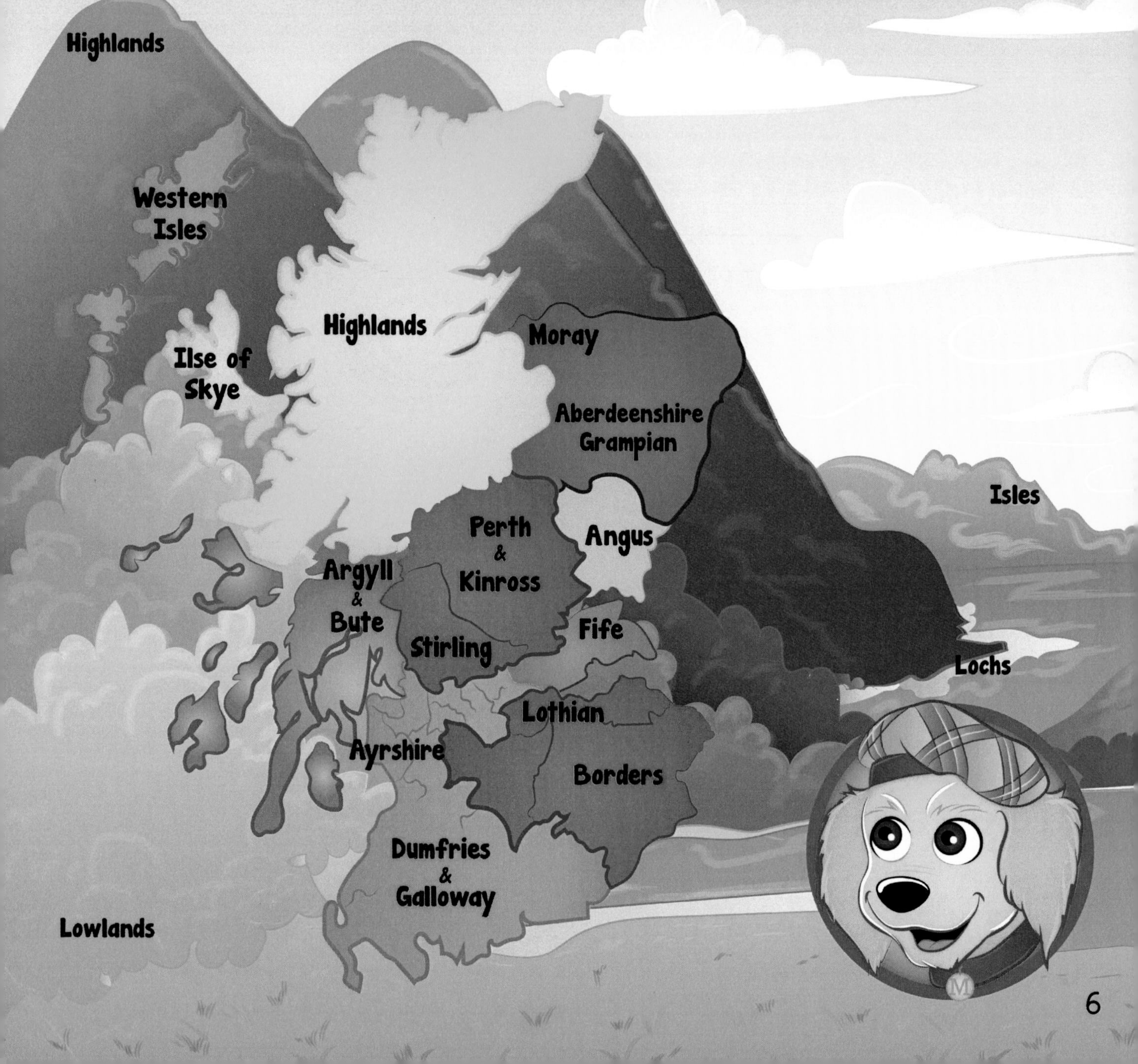

Highlands

Western Isles

Highlands

Ilse of Skye

Moray

Aberdeenshire Grampian

Isles

Perth & Kinross

Angus

Argyll & Bute

Stirling

Fife

Lochs

Lothian

Ayrshire

Borders

Dumfries & Galloway

Lowlands

6

It's a great place for a family.
Together, we explored the beautiful **uplands** and **lowlands**. We went
swimming in the **lochs** and around the **islands** of the North Sea.
We did everything together.

Meet Mom and Dad. They are **responsible** for all of us and teach us to do our best in everything we do. Would you like to meet the rest of my family?

1 Grandmother

2 Sisters

3 Brothers

4 Aunts and Uncles

5 Cousins

We are a pack.

Malcolm, Murray, and Maddox are the best brothers a dog could ask for! They always think before they speak, finish their work before they play, and do their best to be kind to others each day. Maddox always says, "**Character** is the way you really are. It's what you do when no one is watching." He is the best!

Meet Maddy and Blair, always helping others, kind, and fair.
I call them my sisters, even though our moms are not the same.
Dad says, "The ones you love are your family."

Aunt Sandy and Uncle Doug, Cousin Dewey,
Zoey, and Shaw never like to be alone, and
I don't think that is a **flaw**.

Uncle Peyton and Aunt Torts taught me how to play sports.
Cousin Scout, Rolf, and Aunt Millie were always on my team.
Life in Scotland was a dream.
Do you have a large family?

One of the hardest things I ever had to do was leave Scotland,
but life is an adventure.
My Mom told me before I left that I had to become **socialized**.
She said, "The more people you meet, places you see, sounds you
hear, and things you smell, the happier and nicer you will be."

I did what I was told.
I practiced all my lessons, and I passed all my tests,
so get ready, I am on my way!

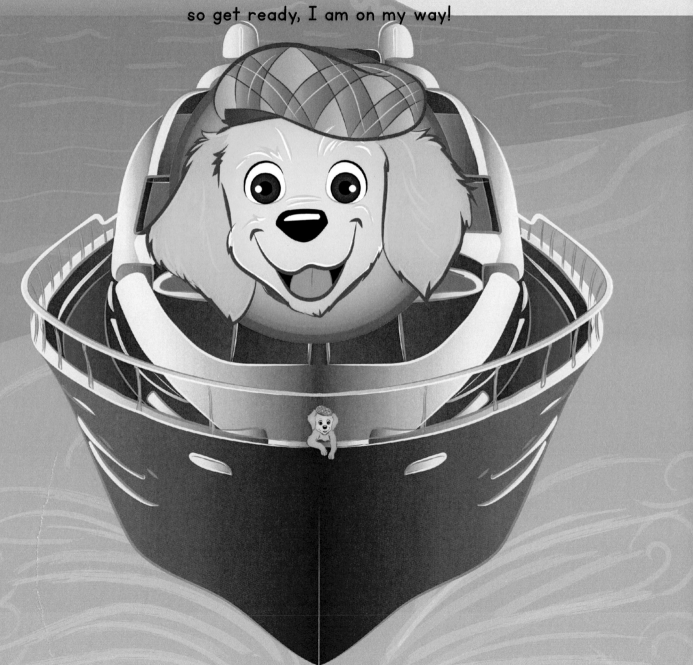

Where do you live?

GREENLAND (DENMARK)

ALASKA (USA)

ICELAND

FAROE ISLANDS

CANADA

IRELAND UNITED KINGDOM

FRA

SPAIN

PORTUGAL

UNITED STATES OF AMERICA

AZORES (PORTUGAL)

MOROCCO

MADEIRA ISLAND (PORTUGAL)

ALGE

CANARY ISLANDS (SPAIN)

MEXICO

MAURITANIA

MALI

CLIPPERTON ISLANDS (USA)

CAPE VERDE

THE BAHAMAS

CUBA

SAINT KITTS AND NEVIS

SENEGAL

THE GAMBIA

BURKINA FASO

GUATEMALA

HONDURAS

DOMINICA

GUINEA-BISSAU

GUINEA

SAINT LUCIA

BARBADOS

SIERRA LEONE

COTE D'IVOIRE

GHANA

EL SALVADOR

HONDURAS

TRINIDAD AND TOBAGO

LIBERIA

COSTA RICA

VENEZUELA

PANAMA

GUYANA

SURINAME

FRENCH GUIANA

COLOMBIA

GALAPAGOS

ECUADOR

BRAZIL

PERU

BOLIVIA

PARAGUAY

CHILE

URUGUAY

ARGENTINA

FALKLAND ISLANDS (UK)

SOUTH GEORGIA (UK)

16

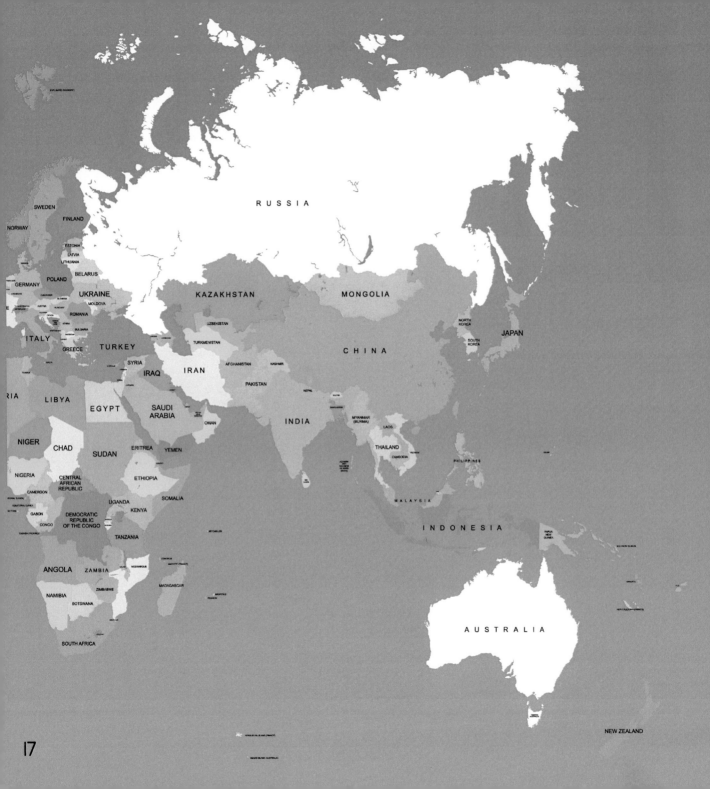

17

Can you find it on this map, too?

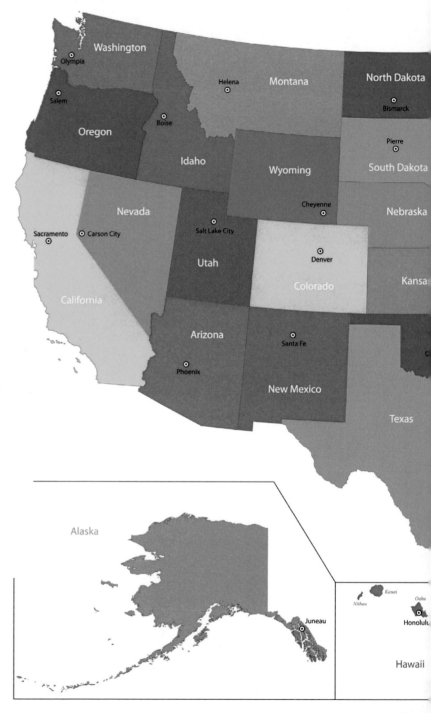

Minnesota
Saint Paul
Wisconsin
Madison
Michigan
Lansing
Iowa
Des Moines
Lincoln
Illinois
Springfield
Indiana
Indianapolis
Ohio
Columbus
Missouri
Jefferson City
Topeka
Oklahoma
Oklahoma City
Arkansas
Little Rock
Tennessee
Nashville
Kentucky
Frankfort
West Virginia
Charleston
Virginia
Richmond
North Carolina
Raleigh
South Carolina
Columbia
Georgia
Atlanta
Alabama
Montgomery
Mississippi
Jackson
Louisiana
Baton Rouge
Austin
Tallahassee
Florida

Maine
Augusta
Vermont
Montpelier
Concord — New Hampshire
Albany
Boston
New York
Providence — Massachusetts
Hartford — Rhode Island
— Connecticut
Pennsylvania
Harrisburg
Trenton — New Jersey
Annapolis
Dover — Delaware
— Maryland
Washington, D.C.

Molokai
Maui
Lanai
Kahoolawe
Hawaii
lu

It takes **effort** to help me stay healthy and safe.
You will need to practice the best ways to **feed, groom, train,** and **exercise** me, but I know you can do it.
Don't worry if you make a mistake.
I will still be your friend, and we can try again.

Dad always says, "The best dog owners are responsible and think before they act."

So here are some rules you will have to follow if you are going to be responsible for me. I know you have my back. You are amazing!

21

I like to eat dog food before we go for a walk in the morning, while you are eating lunch at school, and when you get home at night.

When Maddox was a puppy, he ate so fast my Mom had to put a clean, large rock in the middle of his bowl to slow him down. "It's better for his tummy," she said.

Be Careful!
When I am eating please do NOT:
- Stare into my eyes
- Take my food before I am finished
- Put your hands near my mouth

I might bite you if you are not responsible and safe.

22

A **veterinarian** will weigh me so you know exactly how much to feed me.
Feed me 1/2 of a cup until I am 12 weeks old.

Feed me 3/4 of a cup until I am 12 months old.

1 CUP

3/4 CUP

1/2 CUP

1/4 CUP

I like treats and they can be vegetables, too!

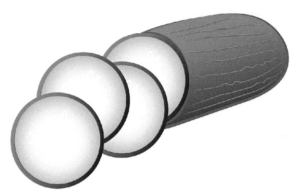

Cucumbers

Green Beans

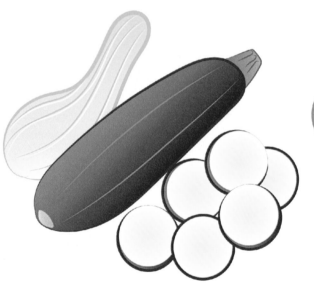

Squash and Zuchinni

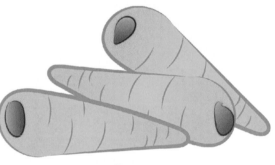

Carrots

They are so good for us.
Do you like to eat vegetables?

Some foods can be good for you, but not for me.
I will eat anything you give me. I might even eat food you don't
give me. These foods can make me sick!

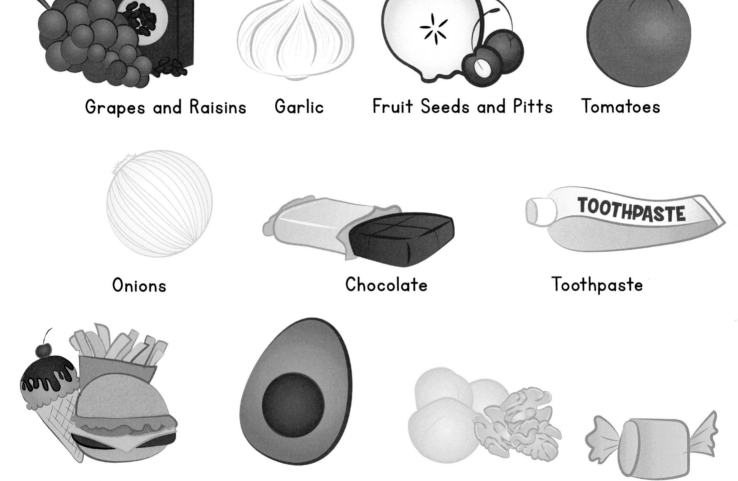

Grapes and Raisins   Garlic   Fruit Seeds and Pitts   Tomatoes

Onions   Chocolate   Toothpaste

Junk Food   Avocados   Macadamia and Walnuts   Gum and Candy

One time, my sister Maddy knocked over the garbage can. I
thought she was so nice to share all the goodies with me. *Yummy!*
It turned out to be a big mistake to eat the trash.
My tummy hurt all night.

Dad was not happy with us. He **growled** about the mess we made, and he had to pick up every bit. Mom said, *"It's better if we keep the food up high and in **containers** so you can't reach it."*

Please be patient with me. Sometimes, I make messes. Puppies and kids make mistakes when they are learning, but we can learn how to do better together.

Toys are my favorite!

A soft toy! A newspaper!
A smelly sock!
I like to take a toy with me
everywhere I go.
This is my football. Please don't let
me lose my football.

28

Guess what?!

When I am being **brushed**, I like to chew on my football.
It keeps me from wiggling away so you can get your job done.
It is a very important job.

I have to be brushed at least three days out of the week.
There are seven days in a week and each day has a name.

Sunday

Monday

Tuesday

Wednesday

Thursday

Friday

Saturday

Which three days will you brush me?

I **shed** my coat every day. Brushing keeps my coat free of **tangles** and hair off the couch, the floors, and out from under the bed and away from the doors.
Do you know how to
vacuum and sweep?
You can learn.
I believe in you.

Clean ✓
Vaccum
Dust
Mop
Sweep

Learning is my favorite!

We can learn to do our best together. Talk to me softly when I am walking, drinking, playing, or sitting.

When you take me to the park say, **"Park."**

When I stick my head out of the car window say, **"Window."**

When you take me outside to go the bathroom say, **"Go potty."**

32

I can learn up to 150 different words,
so please make a list of all of the words
that you are going to teach me.
The more words I know, the smarter
I will be and the more tricks
I will do with glee.

Sit
Stay
Window
Park

Adults must be with us when you are learning how to train me and when we are making new friends. I love making new friends! Please tell them that I do NOT like to be **teased**, poked, or to have my tail pulled.

Be careful! I might bite if I am growling, if I am backing up, or if I am showing my teeth.

The best way to introduce me to new people is to ask our friends to **squat** down, turn a little to the side, and pat their **thighs**. When I am ready to meet them, I will **sniff** and lean toward their legs.

I like it best when my friends are kind and play with me.
I love to play! It is my favorite part of the day.
I don't want you to get hurt so stand up big and tall, and I will try
not to make you fall. If you teach me, I will do as you wish.
We can run or play **fetch**. I will even dress up; I am quite a **catch**.

Exercise is my favorite!

I am at my best after I exercise. It is almost as good as a treat! If I don't get enough exercise, I might break something, even chew on your favorite thing.

One time, I got my head stuck in a ring. I hope I don't do that again. Will you run and play with me for at least one hour every day?

I am so excited that you said, "Yes!"
You are going to be a responsible dog owner and my new best friend!

I want to go everywhere you go, but right now, I am really sleepy.
Thank you for learning how to take care of me.
I am so happy you are now a part of my big and happy family.

Love,
Max

Resources

Glossary

Achievement: Something that has been done or gained through effort: a result of hard work.

Brush: At least 3 to 5 times a week using a bristle slicker brush from the pet store to keep the Golden Retriever's coat clean, prevent knots, and to reduce shedding. Start near the head and work toward the tail. (Ask an adult for help.)

Brush (my teeth): Use a soft toothbrush and toothpaste for dogs only. Lift the dog's lips and gently brush the teeth once a day. (Ask an adult for help.)

Catch: A spectacular find, as in a great partner for a relationship.

Coat: The outer covering of fur, hair, or wool on an animal. Golden Retriever's have a double, water-repellant coat that sheds seasonally and needs regular brushing. The color ranges from light to dark gold.

Container: An object (such as a box or can) that can hold something. Use a container with a lid.

Earth: The planet we live on. Earth is the third planet from the sun.

Exercise: Moving the body so it will be healthy and strong.

Feed: To give food.

Fetch: To go after something and bring it back.

Flaw: An imperfection or weakness.

Golden Retriever: An active and energetic sporting dog that requires daily exercise. They are friendly and always eager to please.

Groom: To keep clean and healthy. Golden Retrievers shed in the spring and fall seasons.

Growled: A low or harsh rumbling sound that comes from the throat of a dog when he or she is mad.

Guest: A person or animal invited to someone's home or activity.

Loch: A lake.

Lowland: Land that is below the sea level and not around mountains or large hills.

Glossary

Pack: A group of animals that hunt and run together.

Patient: Able to wait without getting mad.

Responsible: 1. Having a job or duty dealing with taking care of someone or something. **2.** Able to be trusted to do what is right or to do the things that are expected or required. **3.** Involves important duties, decisions, etc., that you are trusted to do.

Scotland: A division of the United Kingdom of Great Britain and Northern Ireland. Population is around 5,000,0000 people.

Sniff: Bring air into the nose to figure out what is being smelled.

Socialize: To teach someone to behave in a way that is friendly and allowed in society.

Society: The people living together in a country, state, town, or community that share the same laws, traditions, and values.

Sore: A painful spot on the body.

Squat: To lower to the ground by bending the knees so the backs of the feet are almost touching a person's backside.

Tangle: Another word for knots or matting.

Tease: Making fun of or pretending to give someone something and then taking it away. Poking, pinching, or pulling a dog/puppy's tail, ears, or body.

Thigh: The part of the leg that is above the knee.

Train: To teach a skill or behavior by giving directions and practicing over a period of time.

Upland: A region of high land far away from the sea.

Value: A strong belief about what is important or acceptable.

Veterinarian: Doctors who take care of animals when they are sick or hurt, and keeps them safe and healthy.

Feeding Chart
Golden Retriever Puppy

As a rule of thumb puppies require:

Puppies should stay with the mother until **6 weeks** (**8 weeks** is better)

Four meals a day from six weeks to three months (can be three if it works better with your schedule)

3 meals a day from 3 months to 6 months   **2 meals a day after that**

Puppy Weight in Pounds	Weaning to 3 Months	4 to 6 Months	7 to 12 Months	Over 12 Months
AMOUNT TO FEED IN CUPS PER DAY				
3 to 5	1/2 to 3/4	3/4 to 1		
5 to 10	3/4 to 1 1/2	1 to 2		
10 to 20	1 1/2 to 2 1/2	2 to 3	1 1/2 to 2 1/2	
20 to 30	3 1/2 to 5	2 1/2 to 3 1/2	2 to 2 1/2	
30 to 40		3 1/2 to 4 1//2	2 1/4 to 2 1/2	
40 to 60		4 1/2 to 5 1/2	3 1/4 to 4 1/4	2 1/2 to 3 1/4
60 to 80		5 1/2 to 6 1/2	4 1/4 to 5	3 1/4 to 4
80 to 100			4 1/2 to 5 1/2	4 to 4 1/2
100 to 120			5 1/2 to 6 1/2	4 1/2 to 5 1//2
120 to 140			6 to 6 1/2	5 1/2 to 6 1/4
140 to 160			6 1/2 to 7 1/2	6 1/4 to 6 3/4
160 to 180				6 3/4 to 7 1/2

The chart is only a guideline

When switching to adult dog food, do it slowly over the course of one to two weeks by gradually mixing in increasing amounts of the adult food with decreasing amounts of puppy food to minimize stomach upset.

Less Exercise = Less Food

If he/she gets too fat, cut back. If he/she gets too slim, add a bit more.

Educational Resources

The Loved Dog
The Playful, Nonaggressive Way To Teach Your Dog Good Behavior
by Tamar Geller

American Kennel Club
www.akc.org/breeds/golden_retriever

Golden Retriever Club of Scotland
www.goldenretrieverclubofscotland.com

The Daily Puppy
www.dailypuppy.com

Dog Channel
www.dogchannel.com

Your Pure Breed Puppy
www.yourpurebredpuppy.com

Pet Wave
www.petwave.com

Character Counts
www.charactercounts.org

Author

A.J. Richards has always been surrounded by animals: dogs, cats,
horses, hamsters, and even deer to name a few. From an early age, she began
caring for numerous shelter pets and continued into adulthood.
She earned a BA in American Literature and a MA in Public Administration while
working with at-risk youth for a Nebraska non-profit.
She now lives in Berkeley, California.

Illustrator

Rayah Jaymes is an illustrator, chef and musician that comes from an incredibly
large multicultral family which continues to inspire her art and story telling.
She aspires to illustrate many more books that educate
children and their parents about the diverse world around them and how they can
make it better everyday in everything they do.

Find her and more of her books at www.vcartist.com

More Books from A Puppy's New Home

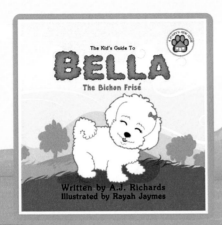

Coming Soon

Made in the USA
San Bernardino, CA
10 June 2015